CONTENTS

Scan this page to download all the audios and videos you need in this module

OUR FOCUS THIS WEEK:

Finding out about the place, the people and how to fit in!

BUILDING THE PROJECT

STAGE 1 — Getting started

STAGE 2 — How's it going?

STAGE 3 — Working together

STAGE 4 — Putting it together

STAGE 5 — Sharing what you did

1

DAY 1

BEFORE YOU BEGIN...

Find out what your neighbour did before class this morning.

1 DIVING INTO DAILY LIFE

Look at the photos.
Label them with as many words as you can.

2 CLOSE UP

Look at the photos again.

Which ones look
- the same as life at home?
- different? In what ways?

What are the best things about daily life at home? Any of these?

school   friends   sport   pets   family   weekends
chores   hobbies   my room   home   studies

The most boring? The most important? Why?

3 GETTING TO KNOW NEW PEOPLE: ASKING QUESTIONS

Add the question words: *What, Why, Which, Who.*

1. _____ did you choose as the best thing?

2. _____ did you choose it?

3. _____ is the most boring thing on the list?

4. _____ is your reason?

5. _____ are your favourite and least favourite times of day?

6. _____ do you like talking to at home?

7. _____ do you like about the place where you are staying?

Think about the answers for yourself.
Now use the questions with your classmates.
Make notes about them here.

Name	Information

Compare the results. Any surprises?

4 PHOTO CHECK

Choose 3 photos on your phone showing daily life at home.

Compare these with other people.

What's the same? What's different?

5 DAILY ROUTINES

Here are two blog posts about daily life here.

Weekday life?

Are you ever late for school? My house is just 5 minutes' walk from school. It starts just before 9am every day, but I often have to run to arrive on time! Why is that?

I get up, do my paper round, have breakfast, and then have a shower. Then I run to school! I take a packed lunch, because I like hanging out with my friends at lunchtime. Sometimes we play football.

After school? I go to swimming lessons at the local pool, or I go to bhangra, to keep fit. Then I do my homework after tea.

After that? Well, I watch TV in the living room, or perhaps some videos on my phone. Nothing special. What about you?

Ben, 15

We have quite a long school day: 6 hours every day, with 7 on Thursdays. That's when we have Public Speaking. So it's quite a long day. I have breakfast with Mum in the kitchen. Then I grab a banana and cycle to school. If it's raining, I get the bus, but I like cycling with my mates. The banana is for the break, in the middle of the morning.

My friends and I have lunch in the school cafe (it's not bad!) and then there's one more lesson in the afternoon. We often go to the library for after-school. Then I go home and do chores like the dishes, or cutting the grass.

What else do I do on weekdays? Well, I talk to my dad on the phone, I do a bit of homework or revision, and I go to my room - my favourite place.

What's your weekday like? Is it like mine?

Kirstie, 16

Which things are similar to your weekdays at home?
Which ones are different?

Read the posts again.
Find key words and phrases to put in these categories.

SCHOOL	ACTIVITIES	TIME

6 CLASS CHECK

Look at the blog posts again.
Which of these questions did each person answer?
Any surprises in their answers?

- How far is it from your home to school?
- When do you start school?
- How long is your school day?
- How do you get to school?
- Who do you have breakfast with?
- What do you do before school?
- What kind of lunch do you have?
- Where do you have it?
- What do you do after school?
- When do you do your homework?
- How do you spend your evenings?

Find similarities and differences to your own daily routines.

7 LANGUAGE FOCUS: WH- QUESTIONS

 Look at these questions. Notice the question words.

- What's the best thing about your daily life? Why is that?
- When do you go to school?
- How many words can you write?
- Which ones are different?
- How long is your school day?

- How do you spend your evening?
- Who do you have breakfast with?
- Where do you have it?
- Who makes your packed lunch?

Now complete these question words.

Wh_____? (place)   Wh_____? (people)   Wh_____? (things or concepts)

_____w? (manner)   Wh_____? (possession)   Wh_____? (reason)

How _____? (length of time)   How _____? (distance)   How _____? (price)

How _____? or How _____? (quantity)   How _____? (age)

 **Remember!**

Except for 'how', question words begin with 'wh' (that's why they are called wh-questions!). Usually a question starts with these words, so you have time to prepare an answer. Use a wh-question to ask for information. The answer cannot be *yes* or *no*.

In spoken questions of this type, the voice often goes down at the end.

PRACTISE

Say the questions above. Ask your partner to check them.

8 CHECK

Check these questions. Are they correct? Why / Why not?

a. Who did I leave my bike?   Correct / Not correct. Reason:

b. When are you going to the library?   Correct / Not correct. Reason:

c. Why are you going to the library?   Correct / Not correct. Reason:

d. How long are you staying at the library?   Correct / Not correct. Reason:

Put these questions in order. Then ask your partner the questions about daily life.

hang out / Who / at weekends / do / with / you ?   Who do you hang out with at weekends?

on Saturdays / you / do / When / get up ?   _____

do / have lunch / Where / you / on Sundays ?   _____

How / sleep / at the weekend / hours / many / you / do ?   _____

the worst thing / is / about weekends / What ?   _____

prefer / Which day / at weekends / do / you ?   _____

TIME CHECK

What's the exact time here now? Check your phone.

What's the time at home? Check that too.

Compare the differences.

10 TELLING THE TIME

You know how to say 'What's the time?'.

But listen to these different ways of asking the time.

> Have you got the time?

> What time is it?

> Any idea what time it is?

> Could you tell me the time, please?

How many times do you hear each one? Think of different ways to answer the time questions.

> **TIP**
>
> We often run words together when we're talking.
>
> What's the time > Wossa time?   What time is it? > Wot time izzit?
>
> **Can you think of other examples. Practise them!**

Use some of these words in your responses.

coming eight yes must
after almost to watch sorry nine
nearly quarter got o'clock haven't ten
half past just thirty about three fifty-four
be up four

Listen and check your ideas.

11 ROLE PLAY

Use these prompts to ask and answer questions about time and events.

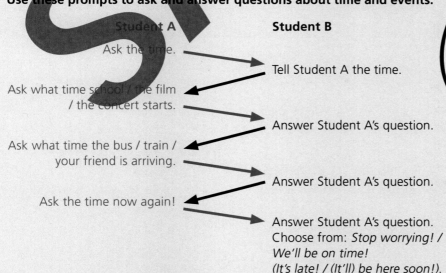

Student A	Student B
Ask the time.	Tell Student A the time.
Ask what time school / the film / the concert starts.	Answer Student A's question.
Ask what time the bus / train / your friend is arriving.	Answer Student A's question.
Ask the time now again!	Answer Student A's question. Choose from: *Stop worrying! / We'll be on time! (It's late! / (It'll) be here soon!).*

Choose different people and situations. Create another conversation.

LISTEN UP!

Notice where and when you hear different ways of asking the time outside the classroom.

Make a note in your journal.

12 CLASS CHECK: SIMILARITIES AND DIFFERENCES

What's your daily schedule here and at home?

Compare this with your classmates.

5

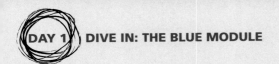

13 WHAT'S HAPPENING?

What's the story?
What do you think
the girl on the left
is asking?

Make notes here.

Try out your questions with a partner.
Add some possible answers.

 **TIP** Look at pages 2-5 again.
Use any useful language.

Write your own conversation about experiences.

14 WHAT DO YOU LIKE TO WATCH?

Find out as much as possible about two classmates. Think of some relevant questions to ask them.
Make notes here.

X likes watching films on TV because...

Also enjoys...

All-time favourite show or series...

X watches TV with …

 Write about these classmates in your journal.

THE DAY 1 TO DAY 2 BRIDGE

1 Look back at page 2.
What photos would you choose for a poster about daily life here?

2 What new activities do you want to try here?

3 What daily activities here have you done?
Take some photos.
What's similar to home? What's different?

4 **CHECK IT AND USE IT**
Look at page 4 again. Can you use all these questions words?
What new ways have you discovered for asking the time?

5 What have you discovered about your classmates?
Any surprises?

LANGUAGE LINKS

Take a look at LANGUAGE WORKOUT 1 on page 34. Sharing experiences.

Don't forget LANGUAGE SUPPORT on pages 46-53.

Don't forget to record your ideas in your journal.

THE PROJECT ☞ STAGE 1 Getting started

**Let's get started today on our new project ...
'Finding out about the place, the people and how to fit in'.**

BEFORE WE BEGIN

Our project will help us explore the place where we are staying, meet the people who live here and discover the things that are different from home.

We can then decide how to describe this place to our classmates and to people at home

ORGANISING AND PLANNING

Discuss these things with your group.

Who will be in our group?

What information do we want to include?

Where can we find the information?

How will we present our project? A video? A live presentation?

Who will do what?

USEFUL LANGUAGE

What about doing a .....?
Or how about a .....?
I'd rather do a .....
We could do a .....
We need to get on with it!

You'll need a small notebook to use as a Project Diary.

Keep your notes there.

DAY 2

1 DIVING INTO HOMES

Look at the photos. Do you recognise any of these things?

2 CLOSE UP

Look at the objects again.

kitchen   bedroom   garden   living room

dining room   bathroom   study

Ask the group (and your teacher). Which ones could be ...?

... in your own home?

... in your teacher's home?

... in the place where you are staying?

Don't look at the photos! What details can you remember?

3 SAY IT BETTER!

Listen and practise the pronunciation of these adjectives and verbs.

modern   cosy   old-fashioned   soft   pull   water

switch off   fill   tidy   set   boil   turn on

Match them to the photos. Combine them with things in the photo to make phrases eg. *water the plants.*

Choose a room in the house. Add more useful words for that room.

Write down as many things as possible that you can find there.

Compare your list with another classmate who has chosen the same room. Add new items.

4 VIDEO TIME: SPECULATE

There are five conversations in the video.

What do you think they are about? Where do they take place? Look at the visual clues.

▶ Watch the video on SILENT. Were you correct?

5 VIDEO TIME: PREDICTING AND CHECKING

Predict five phrases in the conversations. Write them here.

Add five adjectives you expect to hear.

_____ _____

_____ _____

_____ _____

_____ _____

_____ _____

▶ Watch with sound. Circle the phrases and adjectives you hear.

If you hear them all, say BINGO!

Can you remember two of the conversations? Write them here.

6 ROLE PLAY

Look at the photos and objects on page 8 again. Imagine them in a house.

One person is a visitor, one person is the house owner.

Create the conversation as you go round the house.

7 TEAM CONTEST

Read this email. Then close your book and listen to your teacher's questions.

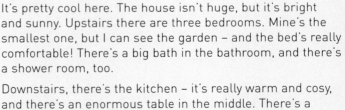

Joe!

Hey there – I've arrived!

It's pretty cool here. The house isn't huge, but it's bright and sunny. Upstairs there are three bedrooms. Mine's the smallest one, but I can see the garden – and the bed's really comfortable! There's a big bath in the bathroom, and there's a shower room, too.

Downstairs, there's the kitchen – it's really warm and cosy, and there's an enormous table in the middle. There's a sofa in there, too! There's a living room and a small study downstairs, too.

The whole house has got carpets and curtains – and there's a garden, too! It isn't very big, but there's a table and a couple of chairs.

So – a pretty nice house! I'll send you more photos tomorrow.

What's your exchange place like?

H

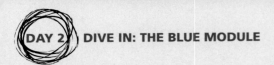

8 | LANGUAGE FOCUS: USING ADJECTIVES

(Abc) POSITION, FORM AND ORDER

Circle the 3 true statements about English adjectives.

Cross out the 3 false ones.

1. a. You put them after *to be* or after a noun.　　b. You put them after *to be* but in front of a noun.

2. a. They have only one form.　　b. They have a singular and a plural form.

3. a. When you use 2 adjectives to describe something, put *and* between them.　　b. When you use 2 adjectives to describe something, put *and* between them after *to be*, but a comma (,) between them in front of a noun.

Match the pairs of example sentences below with the rules above.

___ The kitchen is warm and cosy.　　It has a big, orange sofa in it.

___ They have three friendly cats.　　She's friendly, too.

___ The house isn't huge.　　There's an enormous table.

Think about a house you're familiar with.

Write two example sentences for each rule about that house.

You can find lots of adjectives on pages 8-10 to use.

 Remember to use **an** not **a** in front of adjectives that start with a vowel sound!

Compare your sentences.

Find out more about the house your partner has described.

Is it a big house?　　*No, but it's new and comfortable, and it's got big windows.*

 **ONE / ONES**

Sometimes, when you want to use an adjective, you don't want to repeat a noun. For example:

Which **shoes** do you like best?　　The **green** shoes.

Use ONE or ONES instead of repeating the noun.

Which **shoes** do you like best?　　The green **ones**.

Which is your **house**?　　That small, red **one**.

Ask your partner about a house they would like. Reply using *one* or *ones*.

What kind of houses do you like?　　*Not huge ones.*

What kind of bedroom would you like?　　*An awesome, modern, purple one.*

In spoken English, you can use *pretty* to mean *quite, very. It's pretty cool!*

You can use *so* to mean *incredibly. The bed's so comfortable!*

9 ASKING ABOUT HOUSES AND BUILDINGS

INFO CHECK

Look at the house in the photo.

What do you want to find out about it?

Compare your questions with your classmates.

10 LISTEN

Five people are asking important questions about a building.

Listen and write the number of the speaker.

Is there a loo? ___   Where's your bathroom? ___

Excuse me, could you tell me where the toilets are, please? ___

Sorry, do you have a loo, please? ___   Where's the bathroom, please? ___

Listen again. Are they polite, neutral or informal?

Speaker number	Polite	Neutral	Informal

What do you expect the answers to be?

Guess the missing words.

Of _____. Go up the _____ and it's straight _____ you.

It's _____. It's the second door on the _____.

Yes, through that _____ and it's _____ the right.

Yes, of course. Go _____ the stairs and you'll _____ them at the end of the corridor.

_____ the hall, _____ the kitchen.

Listen again.

Did you hear your ideas? Which speakers were at home?

 REMEMBER! You don't need to understand every word! The general message is often enough.

11 CLASS CHECK

a. Write three questions to ask your teacher about the school.

b. Ask your questions and listen to the answers.
   Compare answers with classmates then draw a plan of the school.

c. Ask your partner about the house where they are staying.
   Compare this with your own houses at home.

LISTEN UP!

How often have you heard phrases like the answers in 10?

 Note where you hear them in your Journal.

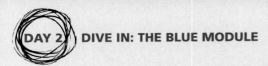

FACTFILE: HOUSES HERE AND THERE

12 DESCRIBING HOUSES

Read this description of a typical house you have seen here.

Here in this region, this is a typical house. It's a semi-detached house, with a small garden at the front and a nice back garden. The garden has flowers, a table and some chairs. It hasn't got a garage, but there's space for a car outside.

Inside, there's a carpet in nearly every room, except the bathrooms. There's one bathroom upstairs, and a toilet downstairs. The kitchen is at the back and has a door to the garden. …

Are there any new words in the text above? Write them in the box.

Do you need any new words to describe your house here? Write them in the box.

Draw a plan of your house. Draw arrows pointing to some of the furniture and objects.

Write a description to go with your plan. Write between 75-100 words.

Show your house plan to your classmates and talk about it.

(P) **Use your description to help, but try not to read it out.**

13 YOUR DREAM HOME

Compare your house plan and description with your home region.

What similarities and differences would there be?

Think about your dream house.

Would it be similar or different? In what ways?

THE DAY 2 TO DAY 3 BRIDGE

What do you think about these things?

1 Look back at the photos from today.
Which things can you find at home too?

2 Take a photo of something in the place where you are staying.
Strange? Cool? Funny?

3 Remember the conversations in the cartoon video?
Choose a different situation. Think of 2 crazy characters.
Create a conversation and make it funny.

4 **CHECK IT AND USE IT**

Look at page 10 again. Do you know how to use *one* and *ones*?
Did you learn anything new here? How about *pretty* and *so*?

5 Look at page 11 again. How can you ask questions about this building?
Record some questions on your phone. Get some answers, too!

6 What have you discovered about your classmates today?

LANGUAGE LINKS

Take a look at LANGUAGE WORKOUT 2 on page 35.
Talking about location.

Don't forget LANGUAGE SUPPORT on pages 46-53.

Don't forget to add important things to your journal.

THE PROJECT ☞

STAGE 2 How's it going?

Now let's carry on with our project ...
'Finding out about the place, the people and how to fit in'.

CHECKING THINGS TODAY

Check your Project Diary. Compare your notes with the rest of the group.

Discuss your progress from yesterday. Agree what needs to be done next.

Who's doing what?

How much time do we have?

Are there any problems? Who can help?

Do you want to change anything?

What have you discovered about homes here?

USEFUL LANGUAGE

How about being an editor?
You're good at it!
I'm going to ...
How about you?

Decide these things before you go on to Stage 3. Make notes in your Project Diary.

DAY 3

1 DIVING INTO CELEBRATIONS

Look at the collage.

- Do you recognise the objects and celebrations?
- Do you know their names in English?

Check with your partner.

2 CLOSE UP

Look at the photos carefully.
Talk about the items and the celebrations.
Take it in turns to agree or disagree.

> I love pulling crackers!

> Me too. I love the jokes.

> I don't like fireworks at all.

> Why not? I love them!
> Especially the noisy ones!

Compare your comments with your classmates.

3 CLASS CHECK

Write 5 questions to ask about celebrations at different times of the year.

Do you celebrate _____ ?

Do you ever _____ ?

What sort of _____ do you like _____ when _____ ?

What _____ ?

Where _____ ?

Use your questions with several classmates.
Try to remember their answers.

Tell a new partner about the classmates you spoke to.
Francesco doesn't usually celebrate his birthday, but he has a party when his team wins!

4 INFO CHECK

Look at your questions in 3 again.

Compare with a partner and choose 5 questions.

Use these to ask your teacher about the area where you're staying.

Are celebrations similar or different here and at home? Find out!

5 LET'S CELEBRATE

Here are four blog posts about celebrations. Choose one.
Read your text and match it with the correct image.
Work in a group of 4. Tell the group about it.

A

In my opinion, the best celebration is the last one of the year – and the first!

I'm not sure why, but our family tradition is to have really good Chinese food for dinner. We always eat around half eight, and it's always an awesome meal! Then we play games at the table until nearly twelve.

We put the TV on and listen to Big Ben at midnight – and then we all sing Auld Lang Syne, the traditional song. And hold hands, of course! We watch fireworks from the back garden, and then it's music and party time!

B

My least favourite celebration is Valentine's Day. There are hearts everywhere, and they even decorate the school! People send anonymous cards; they don't sign them, so you don't know who they're from. (Well, mine are always from my Mum – I know her writing.) And they give small gifts, like heart-shaped balloons or chocolates. I don't like it because I never get a real card – it's depressing!

C

I like family celebrations, like birthdays and anniversaries, best. I don't usually hang out with my family much, but I like seeing my cousins when it's someone's birthday. Typically, we all have a big meal together. Sometimes we go to a restaurant – nobody wants to do the dishes after it!

Then we go back to the house and give the presents. And have cake and just hang out. Sometimes we play silly games, too, like 'What's the Film?'.

D

The celebration I don't like much is Halloween. Well, I like the idea of it, but not the actual celebration. There are a lot of plastic pumpkins everywhere, and some people spend a lot of money on fancy dress costumes. I like those, I usually go as a Martian – but I can't eat sugar. And that's a real problem at Halloween. People go around houses and get sweets and cakes, and I can't have anything. It's embarrassing!

Match these verbs with the correct phrase.

do give go have make

_____ a party   _____ a present

_____ a cake   _____ the dishes

_____ trick or treating

Which celebrations are similar to yours?

Which blog posts do you agree with?

6 PARTY POOPER

Choose a celebration you do not like. Find 4-8 words to describe it.

CELEBRATION
USEFUL WORDS

Write a blog post of the celebration and explain why you don't like it. (If you prefer, do this after Language Focus on the next page.)

Compare your choice, description and reasons with your classmates.

What's the most unpopular celebration? Why?

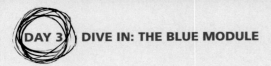
7 LANGUAGE FOCUS: MAKING GENERALISATIONS

 We usually use *the* to refer to something specific: 'the only one' or 'we all know which one(s) we're talking about'.

Leave out THE if you want to make a generalisation. Compare the difference.

> **The** best celebration is the last one of the year = ONE specific celebration.
> **The** celebration I don't like is Halloween. = ONE specific celebration.
> I like family celebrations. = family celebrations in general.

> You can also generalise by using **A** + noun / noun phrase + **verb**.
> *A celebration* **should have music, I think.**
> *A celebration without music* **isn't much fun.**

Look at these sentences. Which ones are wrong? Can you correct them?

- The British people don't usually eat the pies at Thanksgiving because they don't celebrate it!
- A Saint Patrick's Day celebration typically involves a lot of green.
- Relatives at the family birthdays don't always give the presents.

 **When you refer to people in general, use *they* or *you* as the pronoun. *You* is an impersonal pronoun in this context; it doesn't refer to YOU personally!**

*People send anonymous cards – **they** don't sign them, so **you** don't know who **they**'re from.*

You always know when it's going to rain; it's when you leave your umbrella at home!

ADVERBS You can also use adverbs like *typically, generally, generally speaking* and *in general.*

Generally speaking, people eat a lot at most celebrations.

8 HERE AND AT HOME

Think about parties or street parties in your country.

Complete these generalisations about them.

A party generally starts at _____.

Older people – my parent's generation – often _____, but on the whole, they don't

_____.

Parties for young people like me _____.

The best thing about big parties is _____, but on the whole, smaller parties

_____.

In general, what I don't like about a party is _____.

Compare your opinions.

Ask and answer questions to find out more information.

> *On the whole, what do older people do at parties in your country?*

> *I think in general they like dancing to music from when they were young!*

> *Do parties generally begin late in the evening?*

> *No, not always, but, generally speaking, they usually finish very late!*

9 LET'S HAVE A PARTY!

SPECULATING AND CHECKING

You are going to hear 3 conversations about parties.

Before you listen to the conversations, guess the words you expect to hear.

Write them in the boxes.

_____ we have a class party?   _____ need to organise it.

_____ about I ask everyone to bring something?   – Good idea.

_____

_____ someone bring cake?

_____ you give me the recipe, I _____ make one.

_____ will we do about music?

If someone _____ a guitar, I _____ play it.

_____

And _____ about the classroom?

You two _____ tidy it, and we _____ decorate it, OK?

_____

🔊 Listen to the conversations. Were you correct?
Write the missing words in the gaps.

10 ASKING QUESTIONS

SYLLABLES

Read these questions.
How many syllables do you expect to hear in each one?

What about chairs?   How about juice?

🔊 Listen and check.
Listen. How many syllables do you hear?

WORD STRESS

Look at these 2 questions.
Which words do you think are stressed?

Can we have some games?   Can you bring some crisps?

Underline them.

🔊 Listen. Which words are stressed? Say the questions again.

11 ROLE PLAY

You are going to organise a class party.

Decide which things you want for it.

crisps   biscuits   cake   soft drinks
juice   balloons   music   team games
paper cups   spoons   ice cream
chocolate   sandwiches   apples   prizes
decorations   presents

Now choose the ones you can bring, make or organise.

Look at the exchanges in 9. Make two questions and two suggestions about your party.

Organise a party in groups. Ask more questions and make more suggestions.

Can we have some games at the party?

What about prizes?

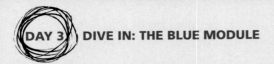

12 **GIVING PRESENTS: A SURVEY**

Find out about presents in different places.

- When do people give presents?
- Do they usually buy them or make them?
- What kind of presents are typical for different celebrations?
- Do young children give things?

Write the results of your survey here.

COUNTRY / PERSON	INFORMATION

13 **PRESENT-GIVING TRADITIONS**

Read this article about traditions in Ireland and the UK.

Children at primary school often make presents for their family. Typical occasions are Mother's Day and Father's Day, and some of the religious festivals.

This depends on the schools and teachers, because there are several religions in each country. For Father's Day or Mother's Day, children usually make a card, or perhaps paper flowers, or a painting.

Teenagers usually give their friends birthday presents. They sometimes give gifts at other times, but these are usually small things. Most don't have much pocket money but, if they are over 16, some of them have weekend jobs. Then they can save money for Christmas and other special events.

In the past, 'Secret Santa' did not exist – it is a new tradition! People in the family, or at work, write their name on a piece of paper. Each person takes one, and keeps the name secret. They buy a small present for that person. So, when you get your 'Secret Santa' present, you do not know who it is from.

Are there any traditions like this in your country?

Check with your classmates.

14 **WORD CHECK**

Find a word in the article for each of these definitions.

This word means more than two or three. _____

This is another way of saying 'a present'. _____

Parents give this regularly to save or to buy something.

_____

This means 'never tell something'. _____

Write any other new words in the box.

15 **WHAT'S YOUR OPINION?**

Is it better to make presents or to buy them?

Making presents is generally better because…

I'm not sure I agree! I think …

What do you think? Do people agree with you?

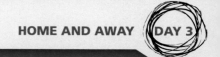

THE DAY 3 TO DAY 4 BRIDGE

What do you think about these things?

1 What have you discovered about different celebrations?

2 CHECK IT AND USE IT
Look at page 16 again.
What did you learn about using *they* or *you* when you talk about people?
Can you make some generalisations about this place?

3 ASKING QUESTIONS: WORD STRESS
Look at page 17 again. Then practise asking questions in a similar way. Record these on your phone.

4 Look at page 18 again.
What did you learn about traditions here and in other places?
Any surprises?

5 Plan a class party.
When? Where? Who? What?

LANGUAGE LINKS

Take a look at LANGUAGE WORKOUT 3 on page 36. Suggesting and negotiating.

Don't forget LANGUAGE SUPPORT on pages 46-53.

Add your ideas to your journal.

THE PROJECT 👉 STAGE 3 Working together

DISCUSSING PROBLEMS AND FINDING SOLUTIONS

CHECKING THINGS TODAY

Check your Project Diary again.
Compare your notes with the rest of the group.
Discuss any problems. Try to find some solutions.
Agree what you need to do for tomorrow.

> How's it going today? Are there any problems? Who can suggest some solutions?

> Do you need to check out new information?

> Have you met any helpful people? What have they suggested?

> Do you have any new ideas about celebrations here?

USEFUL LANGUAGE

Is everything OK?
It's going well / OK / slowly
I have to / need to / ought to + verb
This is a great photo for ...

Discuss these things before you go on to Stage 4. Remember: keep notes in your Project Diary.

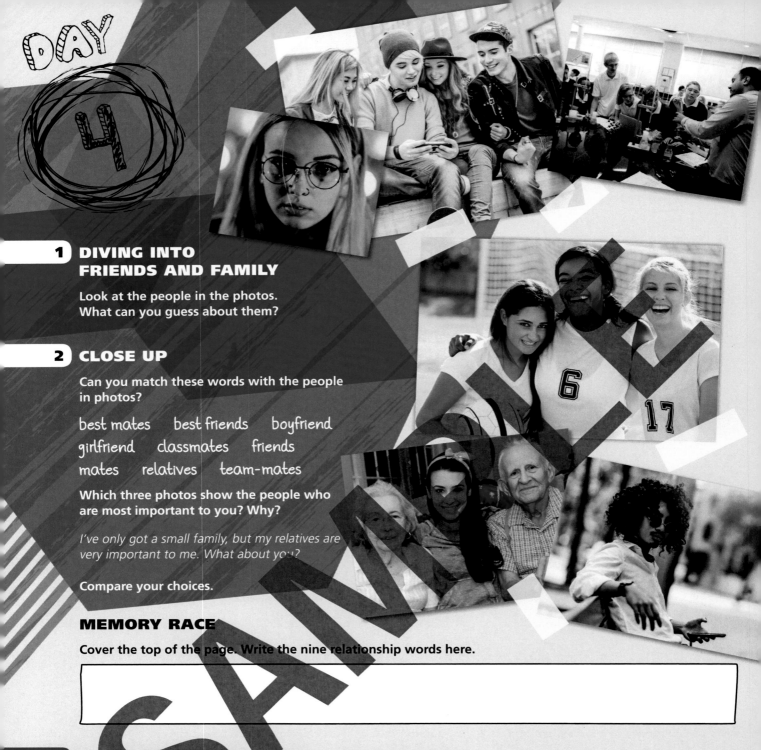

1 DIVING INTO FRIENDS AND FAMILY

Look at the people in the photos.
What can you guess about them?

2 CLOSE UP

Can you match these words with the people in photos?

best mates   best friends   boyfriend
girlfriend   classmates   friends
mates   relatives   team-mates

Which three photos show the people who are most important to you? Why?

I've only got a small family, but my relatives are very important to me. What about you?

Compare your choices.

MEMORY RACE

Cover the top of the page. Write the nine relationship words here.

3 PEOPLE: WHAT ARE THEY REALLY LIKE?

Match these words to the people in the photos.
Some of them describe several people.

beanie   glasses   straight hair   ponytail
cap   dyed hair   curly   wavy hair   headphones

Choose two of the photos. Discuss the people in them with your partner.

Write as many extra words as possible to describe them in detail.

Which of the words above and in the box can you use to describe your classmates? Which ones are new to you?

4 YOUR TURN

Talk about people who are important to you.

Plan what to say and then tell your classmates.

Planning notes

4 **VIDEO TIME: MEETING FRIENDS**

You're going to watch a video.

What do you think it is about? The words in the filmstrip are clues.

weather
neighbours

parties
kids our age
interests
chess

surfing
basketball
summer
smile

You will watch two people talking about meeting friends.

Guess if they will say these ideas are good or bad.

visit the neighbours   go to a club   join a team   do a course
stay with a family with teens   go to a party   shake hands
kiss people on both cheeks   talk about the weather

▶ Watch and check.

There are five mistakes in the video.

▶ Watch it again and find them.

1. _____

2. _____

3. _____

4. _____

5. _____

Choose one of the pieces of advice.

What did the vloggers say? Make a note here.

▶ Watch it again and check.

5 **MEETING ADULTS? HERE'S SOME ADVICE.**

What advice could you give your friends at home about meeting adults here?

Check things on your phone. Ask your teacher

Make a list of important points here.

Dropping in for a visit?

There are a few expressions in English that mean 'visit spontaneously'.

These include *to pop in, to call round, to drop in, to come round, to stop by.* Some of these are generally used by older people, e.g. *pop in.*

In the past, people liked unexpected visitors, but now it's usually better to phone first.

In some places, it's usually a good idea to take a cake or some biscuits.

Expect to drink a lot of tea if you visit adults!

6 LIGHTS, CAMERA, ACTION!

You are going to plan a short video about either:

- Meeting adults here   *or*
- Meeting and making friends here and at home.

a **Look at the notes you made on page 21.**
    Check the language you have practised today.

b **Choose the topic.**
    Write the title: _____

CHECKLIST

Will the video be an interview, a vlog, or a documentary?

Will it be serious or entertaining?

Do you need any props (photos, drawings)?

Key words to include:

Write the script.

Use the one on page 21 to help you.

USEFUL LANGUAGE

Organising materials:

Have we got a …?

Do we need a ….?

How about using ….?

Advice (in the video):

Remember (not) to …

Do try to …

…. is a bad idea!

People feel good / like it if you …

You should always / never …

PRACTISE IT

Ready? Film it with your phone or camera.

When you are happy with it, show it to your teacher and your classmates.

Watch your classmates' videos.

Talk about them.
What did you learn?

7 LANGUAGE FOCUS: DESCRIBING PEOPLE AND THINGS

Look at these red and blue sentences.

Circle the adjectives. Underline the nouns.

Find the word before the noun and draw a box round it.

That looks exciting!	He looks friendly.	She doesn't look very happy.
This sounds terrible!	They sound French.	She sounded happy on the phone.
That looks like my coat.	He looks like my uncle.	They don't look like twins.
This sounds like a Sia song.	You sound exactly like my mother.	She sounds like an actress.

What is the difference between the two groups? Choose the correct statements.

- The red / blue sentences express appearance.
- The red / blue sentences express similarity.

Answer these questions with complete sentences. Use *look* or *sound*.

- Which famous people do two of your classmates look like?
- What or who does your teacher sound like?
- How are you feeling at the moment?
- Who do people say you look like?

 You can also use *seem*, *taste*, *smell*, and *feel* with adjectives or with *like* + noun phrase.

8 SIX-MINUTE RACE

Write as many sentences as possible using *look, sound, taste, smell, feel* and *seem*.

Do not use the same adjective or noun twice. Your sentences must be logical – and polite!

Check a partner's sentences. Are they correct?

Who has the most correct sentences?

WHAT'S IT LIKE HERE?

Write 5 questions about life in the country where you are staying.

Use some of the language from this page.

_____

_____

_____

_____

10 LET'S MEET UP

Look at the cafe signs and check their meaning.
Which ones indicate good places to meet friends?
Which ones are about food and drink?
What can you do in each place?

Ask our staff for today's password

Garden available for customers

More seating available upstairs

Quiet area

Sharing platters

What other useful signs can you find in a cafe? Draw three of them here.

11 GOOD PLACES TO MEET UP

Design a small poster for your school here.

Give information for two good places to meet your friends in this area. Use some of the signs above as 'info-bites'. Add a short description of each place. Explain why you like the place.

Present your poster to the class.

THE DAY 4 TO DAY 5 BRIDGE

More things to think about before the end of this week!

1 Look at page 20 again.
What photos would you choose to represent friends and family?
Can you find any on your phone?

2 What are the best places to meet your friends here?
Take some photos or record your suggestions.

3 CHECK IT AND USE IT
Look at page 23 again.
Can you remember the difference between the red and blue sentences?
Why not make up some of your own?

4 Any advice on making new friends here?

> ### LANGUAGE LINKS
>
> Take a look at LANGUAGE WORKOUT 4 on page 37.
> Expressing ability.
>
> Don't forget LANGUAGE SUPPORT on pages 46-53.

What do other people think?
How's your journal going?

THE PROJECT  STAGE 4 Putting it together

THINKING AHEAD
Check your Project Diary.
Have you decided how to present your Project?
Agree what you need to do before tomorrow.

PREPARING AND PRACTISING
Here are today's check questions. You can add some of your own.

> ### USEFUL LANGUAGE
>
> I don't know how to...
> I'm no good at ...
> Can I work with you?
> How about practising it later?
> Have we got the ....?

> When will you practise the presentation?

> What will you need to present your project?

> Do you need to adjust anything?

> Who will do what?

Get ready for Stage 5 tomorrow!

Update the notes in your Project Diary.

DAY 5

THIS WEEK SO FAR

Write three questions to ask a partner about this week.
They should be interesting or fun.

Exchange books with someone.
Use the questions in the 'borrowed' book to ask classmates about their week.
What have you discovered about your group?

1 DIVING INTO FEELING WELCOME

Look at the photos. Label as many things as you can.
What kind of homes are they? What do you think they are like inside?

2 CLOSE UP

Write down the words you associate with HOME.
Add words for the homes in the photos.

Compare your list with your partner. Do you agree with their choices?

Add any useful words to your list.

Look back at Days 1-4. Find words and phrases there that you can also associate with HOME.

3 BUILDING VOCABULARY

Make a mind map poster about HOME.

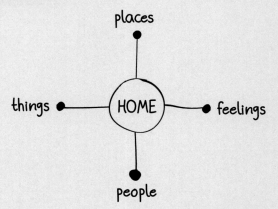

4 WELCOMING PEOPLE

Why is it important to be welcoming to people?

What things can people do to make visitors feel welcome in a place?

Which of your ideas have you found here?

5 BLOG POSTS

Some young people answered two questions on a blog post.

Check out their opinions. Write a short reaction to each one.

What can our home town do to make people feel welcome here?

Why is it important? The most interesting answers will appear in our blog AND win a WELCOME HOME T-shirt!

A

How about giving free language lessons to people who work in shops and cafes? Or even free 'how to speak clearly in English' lessons! Cafe staff – baristas and waiters – often speak very quickly to customers. I think it's sometimes difficult for tourists to understand them! It's important to speak clearly because speaking a foreign language is quite frightening. We don't need to change our accent, but we need to slow down and sometimes choose easier words. Slow English lessons, please!

B

It's important to make visitors feel welcome because we want visitors to get a good impression of our country. We have nice people and beautiful places, but the weather is sometimes grey, so I think we need to smile more at visitors. The sun doesn't always shine, but we can. I think a 'Smile! It's a beautiful day!' poster in every shop and cafe would be fantastic. If people see that, they'll smile. If they smile, they'll feel happier. And visitors will feel welcome.

C

Places with a lot of visitors need a lot of activities like festivals and markets or free museums and art galleries. Tourists are good for our town because they bring money and jobs. But some people come to live here, like refugees or people who change jobs, and we need to be welcoming to them too. It's hard to change your home and go to a new place. We need more street parties and free clubs that meet interests. Clubs for people with children, clubs for teenagers and clubs for adults. We need to say WELCOME HOME!

Compare your reactions.

Choose a heading for each post.

MORE CHILDREN'S ACTIVITIES PLEASE!   SHARE SMILES!   SLOW ENGLISH CLASSES!

SMILES IN EVERY SHOP AND CAFE!   CLUBS FOR EVERYONE   MORE FESTIVALS!

Think of two more ideas. Discuss them with your partner and your classmates.

6 ROOM FOR IMPROVEMENT?

Think about the place where you're staying. What would you change?

Think about your home town. How could it be more welcoming?

	GOOD THINGS TO KEEP OR START	BAD THINGS TO CHANGE OR STOP
Here		
At home		

DAY 5

LOOKING BACK AND CHECKING

It's nearly the end of the week and of this module.
Think about the things you have discovered.

1 Look at the photos on page 26.
What different kinds of homes have you seen here?
What photos of them have you taken?

2 CHECK IT AND USE IT
Look at the blogs on page 27 again.
Suggest ways in which people can feel welcome in a new place.

3 Create a welcome slogan for this town.

LANGUAGE LINKS

Take a quick look at Lexical Support on pages 54-56.

Don't forget to add your own important words.

Share and compare your ideas and suggestions.

THE PROJECT

STAGE 5 — Sharing with others

It's time to present our project ...
'Finding out the place, the people and how to fit in'.

FINAL CHECK
Use the notes in your Project Diary to check everything.
Check with the rest of your group.
Practise your presentation if you can.

GETTING READY, CHECKING AND PRESENTING
Points to check.

Is the script OK?
Who will check
the language?

Do we have all
the photos and
objects?

Is the
technology
working?

OK ... let's go!

USEFUL LANGUAGE

We'd like to present our ...,
to you.
We really recommend ....
We discovered that .....
Thanks for listening.

Now let's see what our classmates thought of it. And take a look at theirs.

THE PROJECT ☞

STAGE 5 Thinking about it all

This week, you have explored HOME AND AWAY.

- in class, with your teacher and classmates.
- out of class, in your group and on your own.

You have used language, photos, and real places and people to do this.
The experience is your personal one!

EVALUATING AND DISCUSSING

How did it go?

What were the comments on it?

What have you learned from doing this project?

What have you learned from looking at the other projects?

Write your review of the project here

OUR PROJECT Things that worked well	Things to think about
OTHER PROJECTS Things that worked well	Things to think about

Was it difficult to comment on the other projects?
What's the best way to do this?

Now wrap up this week on pages 30 and 31.

WRAPPING UP: HOW TO FIT IN HERE

Here are the topics from Days 1-5:

Daily life

Homes

Celebrations

Making friends

Feeling welcome

1 PERSONAL EXPERIENCES

Look at your journal pages again as well as the pages on our day out.

Do these connect to any of these topics? Which ones? How?

Which topics connect most to your classmates' personal experiences?

2 COMMUNICATING

We focussed on some key communication areas.

Asking questions   Talking about routines   Making generalisations   Describing places and things

Talking about experiences   Describing location   Negotiating and suggesting   Expressing ability

Language race: your teacher will choose one area. You have 2 minutes. Work in a team and make a list of words connected with this area.

3 EXPLORING CULTURES

Flick through the module.

Which photos give the best idea of this place?

Suggest a word to describe them. Funny? Awesome? Strange?

Make a note here.

PAGE	PHOTO	CULTURAL INFO	COMMENT

Look at your own photos of this place.

Which ones will you show your friends at home?

We explored different cultures: the local culture here, your own and your classmates'.

What have you learned about your classmates' cultures?

4 MODULE REVIEW

Do a review of this module to inform another class.

Use these criteria, or add your own. 5 stars = excellent!

CRITERIA	ACTIVITY	STARS	COMMENTS
Interest			
Information			
Discussion			
Photos			
Project			
Other			

5 USING THE EXPERIENCE

What are the things from this week's work that you will tell your friends about? Positive and negative!

THE BIG TEAM QUIZ

How fast can your team answer the quiz questions? No cheating! No looking!

 1 Think of another word for…

friend   toilet

_____   _____

call round   gift

_____   _____

bedroom   enormous

_____   _____

family member   studies for exams

_____   _____

turn off (lights)   go by bike

_____   _____

 2 What are they called?

Which of the words do you like best?

 3 Put these sentences in the correct order.

homework my do A. _____
I'll you do and
art your chores _____

blue she's and B. _____
got hair eyes
green big _____

third it's on C. _____
the right
door the _____

are parties fun D. _____
a generally of
speaking lot _____

mate how you E. _____
far live does
best your from _____

pets some like F. _____
people look
their exactly _____

4 Circle the wrong word in each sentence. Then write a better word.

A. How long do you spend making revision before an exam?

_____

B. My best friend lives in a half-house near some of my team-mates.

_____

C. Where do people kiss friends on both faces to say hi?

_____

D. I wear a beanie when I do my paper cup because it's cold when I'm cycling.

_____

5 Write as many words as you can that you've learnt from this module that include the letter E.

YOUR QUIZ!

Your team has to make a new quiz for other teams to try.

Think of at least three kinds of question and write them here and in your team-mates' books.

Keep the correct answers secret!

SHARING EXPERIENCES

1 THINK AND CHECK

Read the questions then choose the correct option.

Have you ever **slept** all morning?

Have you ever **been** to a museum with your school?

Have you ever **wanted** to live in another country?

Have you ever **tried** sushi?

Have you ever **written** a letter?

Have you ever **had** cake for breakfast?

Have you ever asks about: a. a specific time e.g. yesterday   b. your whole life so far   c. your habits

Look at the verb forms in blue. Circle the REGULAR verbs.

How quickly can you remember the past participle form of these verbs?

see _____   meet _____   live _____   buy _____   give _____

lose _____   wear _____   forget _____   leave _____   walk _____

2 THINK AND WRITE

Using the participles above and your own ideas, complete these questions.

Think of interesting things to ask a partner.

Have you ever _____?

Have you ever _____?

Have you ever _____?

Have you ever _____?

SHOWING INTEREST

If your partner answers *Yes, I have,* **you can ask:**

What was it like?   What did you think of it?   Why?

REMEMBER! *What was it like?* and *What did you like?* are very different.

What was it like? **It was great! I loved it! / It was so boring! I hated it.**

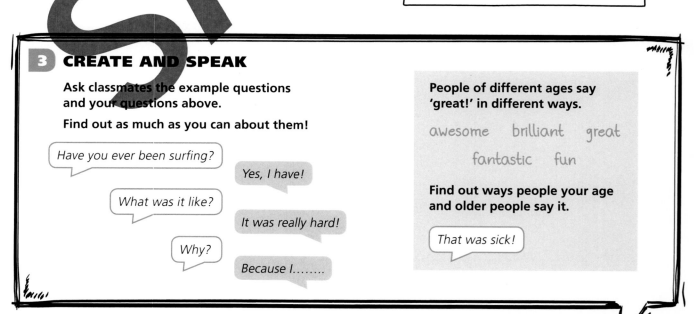

3 CREATE AND SPEAK

Ask classmates the example questions and your questions above.

Find out as much as you can about them!

Have you ever been surfing?

Yes, I have!

What was it like?

It was really hard!

Why?

Because I........

People of different ages say 'great!' in different ways.

awesome   brilliant   great

fantastic   fun

Find out ways people your age and older people say it.

That was sick!

TALKING ABOUT LOCATION

1 **THINK AND CHECK**

Add the letters to the ordinal numbers. Then write them in letters.

1 > 1st - _first_   3 > 3___ - _____   5 > 5___ - _____   12 > 12___ - _____   21 > 21___ - _____

2 > 2 ___ - _____   4 > 4___ - _____   9 > 9___ - _____   20 > 20___ - _____   23 > 23___ - _____

2 **THINK AND WRITE**

Look at the conversation. Put the phrases in the correct place and then practise.

it's   it's got   there's   we haven't got

A: Where can I get a snack?

B: _____ a shop on the second floor.

A: Is there a cafe, too?

B: No, _____ a cafe here.

A: Thanks. How do I find the shop?

B: Go down to the second floor and along the corridor. _____ the fourth door on the left.

A: Cool. Do they sell sandwiches?

B: _____ sandwiches, wraps and pies.

A: Awesome, thanks!

> **TIP** In UK English, the bottom floor is usually the GROUND floor.

3 **CREATE AND SPEAK**

This grid represents a shopping mall. Place these things in the grid.

shoe shop   coffee shop   bookshop   toilets (ladies)   toilets (men's)
restaurant   sandwich bar   cinema   clothes shop (x3)   sports shop

5	4	3	2	1	Shops / floors STAIRS
					4
					3
					2
					1
					Ground

Working with a partner, take turns to ask where things are. Use the grid to help.

Do NOT show your partner your mall.

Listen to your partner explaining where things are. Put them in the grid.

5	4	3	2	1	Shops / floors STAIRS
					4
					3
					2
					1
					Ground

SUGGESTING AND NEGOTIATING

1 THINK AND CHECK

Imagine you are going to buy a gift for your host.

Discuss this with a partner and make a list of ideas.

How about buying a goldfish?

What about getting some tea?

What about finding some flowers?

How about making a video of us?

2 THINK AND WRITE

Read the first two exchanges, and then complete the others.

Can we buy her a goldfish?

If you buy the goldfish, I'll buy a bowl.

Can we get her some tea?

You can get some tea, and I'll get a mug.

Can we get her some _____?

If you get the _____,
I'll _____.

Can we _____?

You can write _____,
and I'll _____.

Remember! These sentences can go the other way round:

If + present tense , will / won't + verb <> *will / won't + verb, if + present tense*

Can + verb + and + will / won't + verb <> *will / won't + verb + and + can + verb*

I'll buy a bowl if you buy the goldfish.   I'll get a mug and you can get some tea.

3 CREATE AND SPEAK

Look at your gift ideas in the box above. Complete these exchanges with your ideas.

Can we buy _____?   If you _____, I'll _____.

Can we get _____?   You can get _____, and I'll get _____.

Can we _____?   We'll get _____ if you _____.

Can we _____?   I'll _____, and you can _____.

Practise your exchanges with a partner.

Now plan five presents you'd like to give your teacher or someone with a birthday in your class.

EXPRESSING ABILITY

1 THINK AND CHECK

Look at this paragraph and at the phrases in blue.

My best friend **can cook really well** and **he's good at learning** languages. He goes running and cycling, and he **can swim** but he **doesn't swim well**. He says he **can't sing** and that he **dances badly**, but **he's ok at it**, really.

Complete the tips with phrases from the paragraph.

Remember!

Tip 1 To express ability, you can use __CAN__ in front of a verb. The negative form is _____

Tip 2 You can also use the adverbs _____ ☺ or _____ ☹ after a verb.

Tip 3 If you prefer, you can also say BE + great / brilliant / _____ / _____ / not very good + _____ + ...ING

Look at the paragraph again. Match the blue phrases to the tips by numbering them 1, 2, or 3.

2 THINK AND WRITE

Complete the following sentences about yourself so that SOME of them are true.

I can _____ quite well.

I _____ quite badly.

I'm extremely good at _____.

I'm not great at _____.

I can't _____ but I'm quite good at _____

People say I _____ well.

Discuss these with a partner. Take turns to guess which sentences are true.
How similar or different are you?

3 CREATE AND SPEAK

Write a short paragraph about one of your friends.
Describe their abilities. Use the expressions above.

Compare your own friends with partners. How similar or different are they?

OUR TRIP OBJECTIVES

FOUR INTERESTING SIGHTS FROM THIS TRIP

FOUR UNUSUAL MEMORIES FROM THIS TRIP

THREE INTERESTING STREET OR PLACE NAMES

STORY TIME

Where? When? Who with? What did I see?

What happened? Why?

What happened as a result? How did it end?

How did I feel? How do I feel about the trip now?

Make a few quick notes here

DOODLE OF THE DAY

OUR TRIP: MORE DETAILS

PICTURE TIME

Take some close-ups for your friends to guess.

QUIZ QUESTIONS

Write 8 questions about some of the things, places and people from the trip.

DON'T SAY THIS!

Choose 3 objects you saw on your trip.

Find 5 words to explain each object.

Make it harder. Classmates are not allowed to use your words in their explanation!

THE PERFECT TRIP – FOR NEXT TIME!

The best things were…

Next time, I think the trip should …

DOODLE OF THE DAY:
This sums it up for me!

 PEOPLE

A person I met today ...

Today I was talking to ...

and ...

Some interesting people.

This is what I remember about them!

More thoughts about the people here.

SAMPLE

LISTEN UP!

What's the funniest thing a person said today?

PLACES

Thoughts about the place where I'm staying.

Good things...

Strange things...

Cool things...

The best places here.

Info for my friends back home.

Places to see again.

LISTEN UP!

Did you have to ask somebody where the toilet was today? What were their instructions?

SAMPLE

WORDS AND PHRASES

These words stick in my mind

because …

The most useful words I've learned …

The strangest words I've learned.

SAMPLE

LISTEN UP!

How many different ways are there to ask the time?
What do the people here say most often?

NOTICES AND SIGNS

Signs here are different from at home!
There are some photos on my phone.

Here are some of them.

Street signs

Public signs

Here in the school

My thoughts about the information in these signs.

MY JOURNAL

THIS WEEK

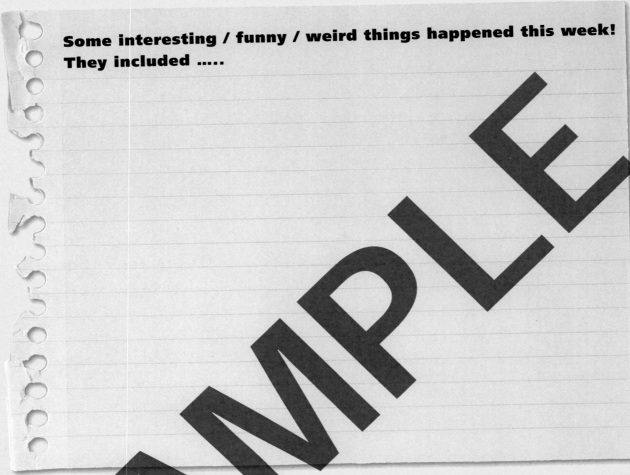

Some interesting / funny / weird things happened this week! They included .....

Some of the new things I've learned this week are .....

MY JOURNAL

What do I feel about this week? Well ...

_____

_____

_____

_____

_____

_____

_____

_____

_____

_____

One word to describe this week?

More thoughts about this week.

LANGUAGE BANK

The language in each module contains a variety of grammatical forms. Some of these reflect the grammatical structure of the English language. Others are functional: they help you communicate in different situations. A third group helps you with vocabulary.

You can use this Language Bank for reference and to help you remember the language you know and have practised. Add your own example sentences or translations to help you remember them.

STRUCTURAL REFERENCE

THE PRESENT TENSE: present simple and present continuous

PRESENT SIMPLE

	Use the present simple …	Your examples
It is five o'clock. Valentine's Day is in February.	to express facts and what is generally accepted as true.	
We usually have cake when it's someone's birthday. Do you always ride your bike to school?	to describe habits (what *always*, *often*, *sometimes*, *never* happens).	
It's the usual story: you forget about your homework until the last minute and then you start to freak out.	for a series of happenings (e.g. in a story).	
Frank doesn't like Halloween.	to express attitudes / feelings.	

PRESENT CONTINUOUS

	Use the present continuous …	Your examples
I'm calling you from Tom's house. Right now it's snowing, and the streets are getting very slippery.	to describe activities / events that are going on at the moment.	
You're doing a lot of reading this year in school!	for temporary situations and actions that don't last long.	

THE PAST TENSE: past simple and past continuous

PAST SIMPLE

	Use the past simple …	Your examples
My little sister was born in 2004. Raoul got to school late yesterday because of the snow.	for completed activities or events in the past (with *dates, yesterday, last year, a year ago* etc.).	
It rained all day. In the evening, Harry wanted to meet friends, so he put on his boots, picked up his umbrella and went outside.	for a series of actions or happenings in the past (e.g. in a story).	

PAST CONTINUOUS

	Use the past continuous …	Your examples
The sun was shining when I cycled home from the swimming pool. While I was walking to school, I saw my friend Amy.	to describe the 'background' to past events, or to say what was happening when another event occurred.	
Everyone was busy. Alice was decorating the room, Hannah was choosing the music and David was baking the cake for the party.	for several activities or happenings all going on at the same time.	

LANGUAGE SUPPORT

THE PRESENT PERFECT

PRESENT PERFECT

	Use the present perfect …	Your examples
I've always hated Halloween. I've had a lot to do since I last mailed you. When are you going to post the letter for grandma? It's been on the table for days.	to talk about something that started in the past but is still continuing today (often with expressions of time such as *always, all week, for* and *since* etc.).	
Have you talked to Ben about the New Year's Eve party yet? She has never forgotten my birthday.	in questions and statements about whether something has taken place (often with expressions of time such *as ever, yet, never, twice* etc.).	
The post has come. I'm afraid the library has just closed. I've forgotten the password.	to stress the result of a past activity on the present (often together with *just, this very moment).*	

IF/WHEN + FIRST CONDITIONAL

	Use the first conditional …	Your examples
If the café has wifi, we can look up the bus times.	to talk about probable future consequences. The structure is: *If/when + simple present, will-future*	
We'll be late for football if the bus is late.	The *if/when* clause can also follow the consequence.	

THE FUTURE

The main forms to talk about the future are the *will-future* and the *going-to-future*.
But it is also possible to use present tenses to talk about the future!

WILL-FUTURE

	Use the will-future …	Your examples
Spurs will win this year. It will probably rain.	for predictions or for something you think is (very) likely to happen.	
I think I'll have lunch at school tomorrow. I'll be there, don't worry.	for spontaneous decisions and promises.	

GOING-TO-FUTURE

	Use the going-to-future …	Your examples
I'm going to build my own house one day. I'm going to bake a cake for the party.	for plans and intentions.	

PRESENT CONTINUOUS

	Use the present continuous …	Your examples
We're visiting London this weekend. I'm playing football on Friday.	for definite arrangements.	

PRESENT SIMPLE

	Use the present simple …	Your examples
Football practice starts at 7.30 pm.	for timetable information.	

LANGUAGE SUPPORT

ADJECTIVES: COMPARISON

ADJECTIVE	COMPARATIVE	SUPERLATIVE	Your examples
Many short adjectives add –er or –est.			
new	newer	newest	
warm	warmer	warmest	
Adjectives which already end in –e add –r or –est.			
large	larger	largest	
nice	nicer	nicest	
Short adjectives which end with a consonant double it.			
big	bigger	biggest	
thin	thinner	thinnest	
Adjectives which end with –y change this to –ier or –iest.			
cosy	cosier	cosiest	
Adjectives with three or more syllables add more or most.			
beautiful	more beautiful	most beautiful	
exciting	more exciting	most exciting	
Some adjectives are irregular.			
good	better	best	
bad	worse	worst	

ASKING QUESTIONS

		Your examples
Where do you live? What did you do at the weekend? Who is that on the photo?	**Wh-questions** begin with a wh-word (*what, who, where, when, which, why*) or *how* and ask for information.	
Do you cycle to school? Have you ever been to a fireworks display?	**Yes / no questions** begin with an auxiliary verb (*do, be, have*).	

COUNTABLE AND UNCOUNTABLE NOUNS

		Your examples
one bottle, a bottle, three bottles one apple, an apple, some apples	**Countable nouns** are things which can be counted. They have a singular and a plural form. You can use numbers and *a/an/some* with them.	
some water some sugar some paper	**Uncountable nouns** do not have a plural form. You cannot use numbers or *a/an* with them.	
a bottle of water a packet of sugar a piece of paper	Often you can use a quantity word with uncountable nouns.	

FUNCTIONAL REFERENCE

You can find more functional language on pages 4, 10, 16 and 23 of this module and also on the Language Workout pages.

Make a note of any other relevant phrases you hear or come across and add them below.

TALKING ABOUT LIKES, DISLIKES AND PREFERENCES	
likes	Your examples
I like … (best / the most / the least).	
I love …	
I enjoy …	
Do you fancy (a coffee / …)?	
My favourite (food / place / …) is …	
I'm keen on …	
… is awesome / cool / great / amazing!	
dislikes	
I don't like …	
I'm not a fan of …	
I'm not keen on …	
I really hate …	
I can't stand …	
… is awful / horrible / disgusting / gross!	
preferences	
You can use *a verb + noun, verb + to infinitive* or *verb + -ing form*	
I prefer black coffee.	
I prefer to drink coffee.	
I prefer swimming (to cycling).	
Do you like dark chocolate? – It's okay, but I prefer milk chocolate.	

LANGUAGE SUPPORT

MAKING REQUESTS

	Your examples
Notice the difference: *I like* = shows preference *I'd like (I would like)* = for requests **You can use *I'd like + noun* or *I'd like + to infinitive***	
What would you like? – I'd like a coffee and a slice of carrot cake, please.	
Could I have some …?	
I'll have today's special, please.	
Would you like some cream with that? – Yes, please. / No, thanks.	
I'd like to go / do / have …	
… and if you're being polite …	
Excuse me, …	
Could I possibly have …?	
I wonder if you could …?	

MAKING SUGGESTIONS AND GIVING ADVICE

	Your examples
Let's …	
How about the blue one?	
How about joining a club?	
Why don't you …?	
We should meet up soon!	
I can recommend …	
You ought to …	
Take your litter with you!	

EXPRESSING ABILITY

	Your examples
She's good at football / keeping secrets.	
I can cook really well.	
I dance really badly.	
Mum can't cook at all, but Dad's a great cook.	

TALKING ABOUT OPINIONS

Stating an opinion	Your examples
I think / believe …	
I am certain / sure that …	
My opinion / view is that …	
I share / don't share your opinion.	
Personally, I think that …	
In my opinion, a vegetarian diet is healthier.	
What's your opinion on this?	
What do you think about / of …?	
How do you feel about that?	
Agreeing	
I totally agree.	
I think you're absolutely right.	
Absolutely!	
Agreed! Cycling is awesome.	
I agree with you 100 %.	
That's so true.	
Disagreeing	
I disagree completely.	
I'm afraid I disagree.	
I don't agree with you.	
Sorry, I think you're wrong. Surfing is much more fun!	
I don't think so.	
No way! *(informal)*	

DESCRIBING PEOPLE, PLACES AND THINGS

	Your examples
It looks / sounds / seems awesome.	
He sounds just like his dad.	
What does it taste like? – It tastes delicious / disgusting / salty / …	
I'm allergic to …	
You're amazing / beautiful!	
It's similar to / identical to …	
He's different from / to his brother.	
The blue shoes are nice. But not as nice as the red ones. And they're nicest in pink!	
Tell me about …	
What's it like?	

celebrations

- festivals
- birthdays
- religious occasions

welcoming people

- at home
- at school
- outside school

SAMPLE

home an

my routine

- time
- meals
- lessons
- interests and hobbies
- homework

describing things

- caramel coffee
- relaxed
- old-fashioned

- my favourite cafe
- the taps in the bathroom

- people
- places
- things
- activities
- feelings

Build your own vocabulary mind map!
Add any new words you see or hear.

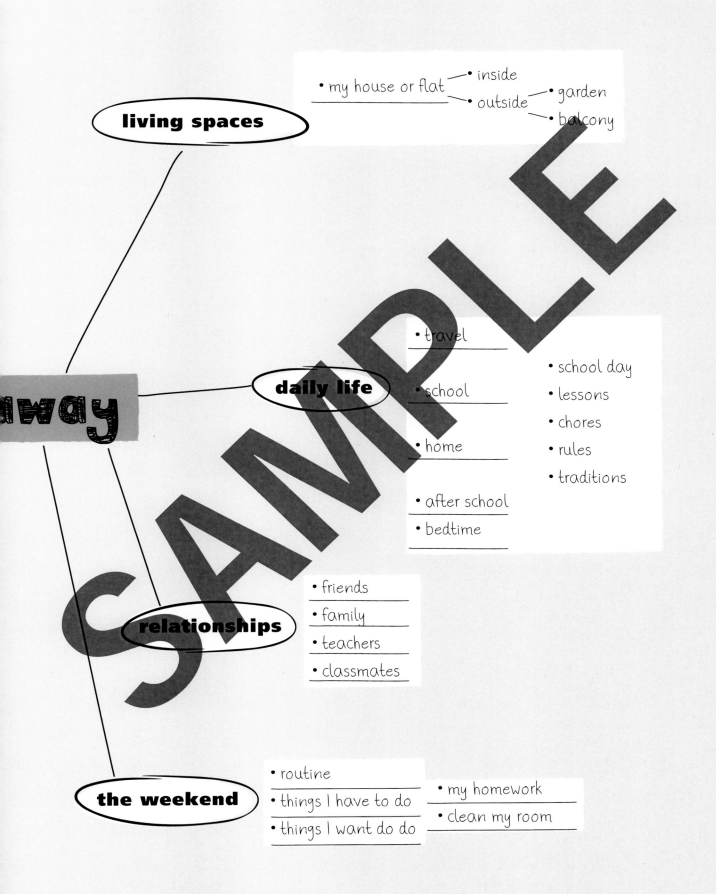

living spaces

- my house or flat
  - inside
  - outside
    - garden
    - balcony

away

daily life

- travel
- school
- home
- after school
- bedtime

- school day
- lessons
- chores
- rules
- traditions

relationships

- friends
- family
- teachers
- classmates

the weekend

- routine
- things I have to do
- things I want do do
  - my homework
  - clean my room

Words from the week.
Think about the week and add words that will help you talk about your time here.

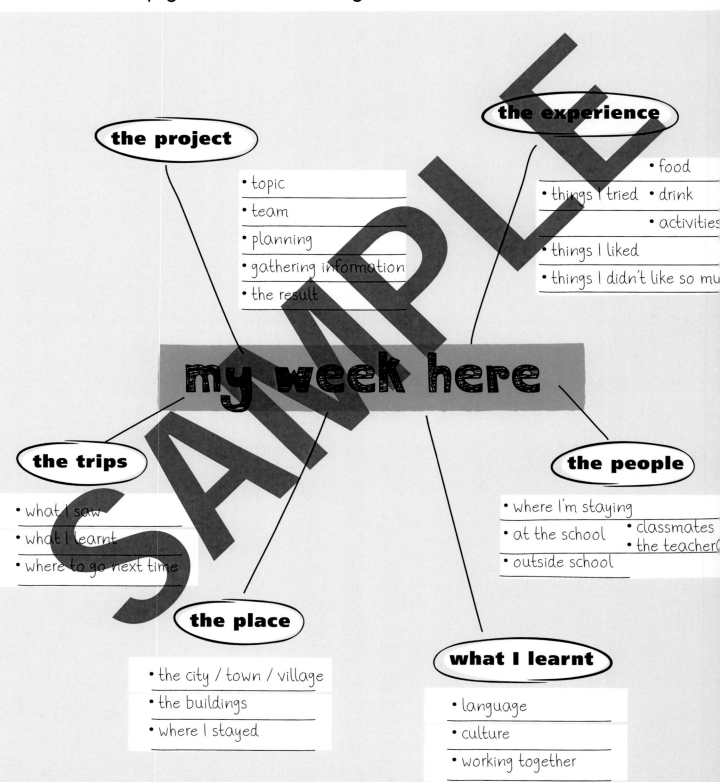

the project
- topic
- team
- planning
- gathering information
- the result

the experience
- things I tried
  - food
  - drink
  - activities
- things I liked
- things I didn't like so mu

my week here

the trips
- what I saw
- what I learnt
- where to go next time

the place
- the city / town / village
- the buildings
- where I stayed

the people
- where I'm staying
- at the school
  - classmates
  - the teacher(
- outside school

what I learnt
- language
- culture
- working together